PUTTING GOD FIRST

A Daily Word with Dr. Ed Young

the **winning** walk®
with **Dr. Ed Young**

Published by The Winning Walk
(The Broadcast Ministry of Second Baptist Church, Houston, Texas)

The Winning Walk

For information contact:
The Winning Walk
P.O. Box 1414
Houston, TX 77251
1.800.946.9255
winningwalk.org
second.org

Printed in the United States of America

978-1-952144-18-9

Dear Friends,

In Proverbs 3:5-6, which has served as my life-verse, we read: Trust in the Lord with all thine heart and lean not unto thine own understanding. In all thy ways acknowledge Him, and He shall direct thy paths. In other words, when we put God first, He gives us direction and guidance along the pathways of our lives.

These selections have been made to help you put God first in your life. They offer illustrations and in-spiration for trusting in the Lord with all your heart and acknowledging Him in all your ways. And if you, and if I, put Him first, He will give us direction and guidance in every decision of our lives.

So let me thank you for using Putting God First as a devotional in your Winning Walk. I pray it will strengthen your existing quiet time with the Lord or perhaps even be the start of a daily devotional habit that will change your life. Along the way, I trust you will discover that God's way works when we put Him first.

His and yours,

Symbols that Teach

**What it means to make a difference
in the world around us.**

*Do not love the world, nor the things
in the world. If anyone loves the world,
the love of the Father is not in him.
– 1 John 2:15*

In the New Testament, there are a number of symbols for the Kingdom of God. Jesus says it is like salt, like light, like water, like leaven, and like a key.

What do these five things have in common? One thing: penetration. Salt penetrates meat to preserve it. Light penetrates darkness to illuminate it. Water penetrates the soil to refresh it. Leaven penetrates dough to help it rise, and a key penetrates a lock to open it.

As Christ-followers, we are not to let the world get into us. But God has placed us in the world for one very clear reason, and that is in order to penetrate our world with the Good News of the Gospel.

A Good Beginning

This book captures the hopes, joys, sorrows, and longings of the human heart.

*O satisfy us in the morning with Thy
loving kindness, that we may sing for joy
and be glad all our days.
– Psalm 90:14*

The book of Psalms is a book of human emotions. Psalms take us into the beauty of the sanctuary where there is worship, and into the painful depths of despair. Psalms express hate and love, fear and faith. When Jonah was in the belly of the fish, he drew his words from the book of Psalms. Jesus in the Upper Room and on the Cross expressed his emotions as he drew from Psalms.

Peter at Pentecost and Paul in Romans both turned to Psalms. Often when we're confused, or life has bottomed out, we have a tendency to talk to ourselves. But I have discovered that when you and I talk to ourselves, we are not talking to someone who is very smart. We can lie to ourselves. It's better to turn to God's Word and allow it to speak to us. And in many of life's most challenging situations, the book of Psalms – the songbook of the Bible – is the best place to begin.

Be Patient

**You can trust God to complete
what He is doing in your life.**

*However, the hair of his head began
to grow again after it was shaved off.
– Judges 16:22*

When Samson revealed the secret of his strength to Delilah, it resulted in his capture and humiliation at the hands of the Philistines. But there is a remarkable verse in this account. We read that Samson's hair began to grow again. That's great news, because it tells us that forgiveness is God's business. But it also tells us that restoration is a process that takes time. Even after forgiveness has taken place, it will take time to rebuild those spiritual disciplines in our lives.

It also takes time to rebuild broken relationships. But don't become impatient about this. Recall that it took time for Samson's hair to grow, and for his commitment to be renewed so that God could use him again. God did use Samson – and He did so in a mighty and powerful way.

Thank God for His more-than-amazing grace, that both forgives – and restores.

The Banquet Table

God gives us what we can never merit or earn.

*For He has satisfied the thirsty soul, and the
hungry soul He has filled with what is good.
– Psalm 107:9*

Years ago, a story in the Boston Globe reported on one of the most dramatic wedding banquets ever. A couple had planned an elaborate banquet for their wedding reception, but two weeks before the wedding the groom broke off their engagement. The bride decided to proceed with the banquet anyway, and she invited all the homeless in Boston to attend. For one evening, they were treated to a tremendous time of feasting and celebration.

When we go to God's great banquet table of grace, we will not be there because we have earned our presence or paid for it.

It was paid for by the sacrifice of another. And the difference, for us, is that the party will go on and on – forever.

God's Drumbeat

**We belong to Christ because we
have been bought with a price.**

*Let a man regard us in this manner, as servants
of Christ, and stewards of the mysteries of God.*
— 1 Corinthians 4:1

When I study the Bible, I look for what I call "pregnant" words that are rich in meaning and that provide extra insight into what God wants us to understand and apply to our lives. In this verse we have one of those words, the word "servant." The word Paul used here is one of the more unusual words for servant in the Greek language. It actually means "under-rower." A Roman warship had a galley where slaves would function as the rowers who propelled the ship. They were completely dependent upon the owner, or the captain, of the ship for direction.

That is how God describes who we are in Christ. We are "under-rowers" and Christ is our Captain, commanding us. We row to the Captain's beat, we submit to the Captain's orders, and we are committed for life to obey our Captain and depend on His direction. We are slaves to the Lord Jesus Christ. But the beauty of it all is that we are thereby allowing Him to supply the music of our lives, and we are depending each day on the cadence of the drumbeat that He supplies.

What is it?

We can trust God for all our daily provisions.

*And my God shall supply all your needs
according to His riches in glory in Christ Jesus.
– Philippians 4:19*

When the Israelites fled Egypt and were making their way to the Promised Land, they lived on an unusual diet. It was called "manna," which means, "What is it?" Manna was God's gift to the people; all they had to do was receive it and trust Him daily to provide it for their food.

Our scripture assures us God has promised to supply all our needs, according to His riches in glory in Christ Jesus...and He does it daily. And, like the Israelites and manna, we can be certain our provision will come from a loving Father, and will be good, plentiful, and nourishing for us. So ask the Father in Heaven to give you this day your daily bread. You can be sure He will deliver everything you need this very day to live for Him.

Say Ahhh!

Our tongues reveal what's in our hearts.

*But no one can tame the tongue; it is
a restless evil and full of deadly poison.
– James 3:8*

When I was a child, our family doctor made house calls. I can still picture Dr. Gatlin entering my room with his black bag. He would first listen to my heart and then take a wooden tongue depressor, tell me to open wide, stick out my tongue and say "Aaah."

Not only does the tongue help reveal our physical ailments, it also helps diagnose our spiritual condition. That's because the tongue is a messenger of the heart and can only deliver the message it is given. Jesus said that the mouth speaks out of that which fills the heart (Matthew 12:34). In fact, nothing reveals what's in our hearts as accurately as our tongues. So open wide and say "Aaah." What is your tongue revealing about the condition of your heart and relationship with the Lord?

Don't Stay Put

When we come to Christ, change takes place.

*Therefore if any man is in Christ he is a
new creature; the old things have passed away;
behold, new things have come.*
– 2 Corinthians 5:17

There is one place God will never let you stay – the place where
you are. Once God touches our lives, we can be certain we will
never be the same. He will move us, change things, even shake us
up to get us where He wants us, because for the Christian, there is
no such thing as status quo.

There is a chorus by musician Ken Medema that always challenges
me: "Will you stay where you are, or will you reach for a star? Play
the game? Be a fraud? Or die to self and live to God? This could
be victory's hour, claim His grace, claim His power. Will you stay
where you are, or reach for a star?"

Is God calling you to change something in your life? Don't stay put.
Reach for a star – the Star, Jesus Christ – and let Him take you to
new heights.

Putting God to the Test

**When we are faithful in our giving,
we discover we can't outgive God!**

*"Bring the whole tithe into the storehouse, so that there
may be food in My house, and test Me now in this," says
the Lord of hosts, "if I will not open for you the windows of
heaven and pour out for you a blessing until it overflows."
– Malachi 3:10*

The Bible teaches that we are not to test God. However, our verse
today has God Himself inviting us to do just that – to put Him to the
test – and it comes regarding our giving. Many things might keep
people from giving faithfully to God. It might be fear or insecurity
in personal finances. It may be a habit, good or bad, that may drain
our income. It may be pure selfishness or greed. We want it all
for ourselves.

Let me encourage you to take God up on His offer. Give cheerfully
to His storehouse, the church, and watch the windows of Heaven
open and pour out a blessing beyond measure. You will discover a
marvelous truth: You cannot outgive God!

God's Kids

God calls us to be childlike, not childish.

And He called a child to Himself and set him before then, and said, "Truly I say to you, unless you are converted and become like children, you will not enter the kingdom of heaven." – Matthew 18:2-3

God loves kids! In fact, children and youth have played vital roles in the Kingdom. "You are not able to go against this Philistine...for you are a youth," were the words David heard just moments before he killed Goliath. Paul urged Timothy to let no one look down on his youthfulness, but to be an example in speech, conduct, love, faith, and purity. And when Jesus wanted an example of the humility, trust and faith necessary to enter the Kingdom of Heaven, "He called a child to Himself."

God calls us to be childlike, but not childish. We're childish when we lack maturity and refuse to grow up. We're childlike when we're humble, trusting, and receptive. One thing is certain, children were attracted to Jesus...and it is still through that childlike faith that people enter the kingdom today.

Hitting Bottom

**When we admit we've hit bottom,
God can begin His healing work.**

*For Thine arrows have sunk deep into me,
and Thy hand has pressed down on me.
– Psalm 38:2*

Psalm 38 is the sound of a man hitting bottom. It was written by King David after his sin with Bathsheba. It records the suffering of sin, the penalty of sin, the loneliness of sin, and the confession of sin.

Healing begins when a person is able to say, "My life is spinning out of control, and I cannot recover on my own power." But because we try to present a spotless image, we find it tough to admit we're out of control. Instead, we try to control life's circumstances and other people. We even try to control God! Isn't it ironic that the way to victory is NOT to maintain control, but to acknowledge we have lost it? Is there an area of your life that is out of control? Admit it to God and let His healing work begin.

The Big Picture

**God works the pieces of our lives
for our good and His glory.**

*And we know that God causes all things to work
together for good to those who love God, to those
who are called according to His purpose.
– Romans 8:28*

A lot of us view life as a jigsaw puzzle. It's as if God has handed us all the pieces and we struggle to make them fit. But God does not see it that way. In this puzzle we call life, He sees the whole even as we fumble with the pieces, and He causes it all to work together for our good and His glory, for those who love Him and are called according to His purpose.

What pieces in your life seem out of place? Which seem to be missing? Thank God that He sees the whole, and is at work in ways we cannot see or understand.

Gone Fishing

Watch out for Satan's lures!

*Submit therefore to God. Resist the devil
and he will flee from you.*
– James 4:7

Did you know the devil loves to fish? He baits his hook with a lure
that is certain to attract us. He's a good fisherman, too. After all,
he's been fishing for hearts and lives since Adam and Eve lived in
the Garden of Eden. He knows where we're vulnerable, and he's
shrewd enough to hide the hook from us until it's too late. Once we
take Satan's bait and the hook is set, we're caught.

The trick to evading the fisherman is to steer clear of the lures. We
can be sure he knows just how to tempt us, but we also have within us the power to overcome temptation, if we'll only use it. Jesus
Christ gives us strength to resist the devil, and when we do, he will
flee! So identify your favorite lures and watch carefully for Satan's
next fishing expedition. Don't take the bait!

Taking Responsibility

**Confession can be an important step
on the path to freedom.**

*Therefore, confess your sins to one another, and pray for
one another, so that you may be healed. The effective
prayer of a righteous man can accomplish much.
– James 5:16*

This verse is the doorway to understanding yourself and understanding others. We confess to others because the Bible com-
mands it, and it has a way of moving us out of the pit in which we
may find ourselves. The thought of confessing to someone may
feel worse than dying, but with the confession there is freedom as
you invite that person to walk around on the holy ground of your
life. Be sure you tell someone who is trustworthy, who can keep
confidences, and who is spiritually mature. Often, you will see
God's grace on the face of the person who is listening to you.

After you have confessed your sin to God, and admitted it to
yourself, confess it to this trusted individual. It's an important step
toward taking responsibility for your actions. When you're ready,
God will lead you to the right person to tell – and He will give you
the words to say.

Fully Devoted

**Don't miss the blessing of receiving
all that God has prepared for you.**

*Be devoted to one another in brotherly love; give
preference to one another in honor; not lagging behind
in diligence, fervent in spirit, serving the Lord; rejoicing
in hope, persevering in tribulation, devoted to prayer.
— Romans 12:10-12*

A country doctor had a sign over his office door that read, "First visit $25. All other visits, $10." A man who was known to be pretty cheap went to see the doctor. He greeted him by saying, "It's good to see you again." The doctor proceeded to examine the man but didn't say anything. When he finished the man was upset and asked what he was supposed to do? The doctor replied, "I want you to do the same thing I told you to do the last time you were here."

God wants us, as His children, to be devoted to prayer. Only when we make prayer a regular discipline can we receive the "just in time" provision He has for us each day.

Drawing Power

**Christ is magnified through our witness
and our walk.**

*According to my earnest expectation and my hope,
that in nothing I shall be ashamed, but that with all
boldness, as always, so now also Christ shall be
magnified in my body, whether it be by life, or by death.
– Philippians 1:20*

Why does Christ need to be magnified by our bodies?

It is almost as though the Apostle Paul is saying, 'My body is a telescope.' When you look through a telescope, a distant star appears to be near. For a lot of people, Jesus Christ is far away, and He appears as some sort of mystical figure you can't understand or really know much about. But, if my body becomes a telescope, it brings Christ near to people who would never see Him unless I, through my body, draw Him. He is far away from some but, through our lifestyle, He becomes near.

Let us, like Paul, pray that Christ would be magnified in and through us.

Graduation

What you live for is evident in the way you live.

Whatever you do, do your work heartily,
as for the Lord rather than for men.
– Colossians 3:23

Every year a certain pastor preached the same sermon to the seniors graduating from high school. He would say, "One day you're going to die. They will dig a hole and put you in it and throw dirt over your face. And at that time everyone will know whether you lived for a title or for a testimony. Pharoah had a title, but Moses had a testimony."

Nebuchadnezzar had a title, but Daniel had a testimony. Herod had a title, but John the Baptist had a testimony. And Pontius Pilate had a title, but my sweet Savior had a testimony."

A good question for all of us to consider today: Are you living for a title, or for a testimony?

No Wiggle Room

Christ must be on center stage in our lives.

*Only conduct yourselves in a manner
worthy of the gospel of Christ.
– Philippians 1:27*

Did you notice the first word in today's verse?

It's the word "only." It means: this one thing you do, this is the most important thing, this is what the Christian life is all about. The word "only" has an exclusivity about it. It means we don't have other options, and we can't say that God's Word isn't clear and direct. Do you want to know how to live each day? In light of your commitment to Christ, this – and this way "only" – is how you live now.

Wouldn't it be wonderful if that word "only" would blink on and off in our Bibles. "Only." "Only." Only conduct yourselves in a manner worthy of the gospel of Christ.

Real Joy

**Happiness depends on circumstances,
but joy depends on God.**

*Make my joy complete by being of the
same mind, maintaining the same love,
united in spirit, intent on one purpose.*
– Philippians 2:2

There are some things in life that are joy takers, and others that are joy givers.

What are some of the joy takers? The first is habits – unhealthy attractions, time robbers, and things that keep us from being sensitive to God. The second is relationships – people with so much bitterness or anger that they suck the life out of you. Now, what are the joy givers? Habits and relationships. The right kind of habits, the right disciplines, and relationships with people who enrich us, challenge us, and listen to us. Which relationship do you think will give us the most joy? You guessed it – it's our relationship with the Lord Jesus Christ.

That is the relationship that will keep on giving us joy, real joy – wonderful joy!

The Cure for Greed

**When we give, greed will loosen its grip
on our hearts.**

*But He said them, "Beware, and be on your guard
against every form of greed, for not even when one has
an abundance does his life consist of his possessions."
– Luke 12:15*

John D. Rockefeller was once asked, "How much money does it take to satisfy somebody?" He famously answered, "Just a little more." No one is immune to greed. A person can have much and be greedy, or a person can have little and be greedy. Jesus says to beware of all forms of greed, because a person is not defined by his possessions or position in life.

What is the cure for greed? The answer may surprise you. Giving! If you are struggling with greed, look for opportunities to be generous and give. Proverbs 11:25 reminds us, "The generous soul will be made rich." The true riches of God are far greater and much deeper than a dollar mark. They will make a difference for eternity.

One of Those Days

God knows just what we need to live for Him today.

He gives power to the weak and
strength to the powerless.
– Isaiah 40:29

Charlie Brown and Lucy were on a cruise ship, and they were setting up their folding chairs on the deck of the ship. Lucy said, "Charlie, some people like to place their chair so they can see where they've been. Some like to position the chair so they can look over the side of the ship. And others like to sit where they can see what's coming. Charlie looked at her and said, "I'm just trying to figure out how to unfold my chair."

Do you have days like that? If so, today's verse provides good news. Just tell God how confused and helpless you feel – He is ready to provide just what you need today – tomorrow – and for the rest of your life.

When God Entered History

**How should you respond when
you get what you expect?**

*And He began to say to them, "Today this
Scripture has been fulfilled in your hearing."
– Luke 4:21*

What if a person claimed to be God, and that person entered this world, what would he be like? That is a valid question. If God entered the world, what would you expect? I think you'd expect an unusual entrance into human life. His birth would be dramatic and different. And you would expect a perfect life, someone who would live without sin. And you would expect this individual to perform miracles. You would expect that this God-man could do as He desired, including the miraculous. You would expect Him to speak the truth, and to answer the spiritual hunger in the hearts of men and women. And you would expect that He would have power over death.

If God has invaded history, and spoken to man, and paid the price for our sin and rebellion, we would expect Him to ask us to align our lives with the principles He taught and to know life – real life, right? Well – He did. And He does.

A Precious Heirloom

**Remember the principles that
make our nation great.**

*Righteousness exalts a nation,
but sin condemns any people.
– Proverbs 14:34*

A little girl asked her mom, "Mommy, do you remember that beautiful vase that is a family heirloom and that has been handed down from generation to generation?" The mother was pleased that the little girl had taken notice of it, and she replied, 'Yes, I am acquainted with that.' The little girl then said, 'Well, Mommy, you will also be interested in knowing that this generation just dropped it!"

We, as Americans, have a heritage, a history, a way of life that has been handed down to us from generation to generation.

As we celebrate this great nation, let us be reminded again of the price that was paid – and that must continue to be paid – to ensure that we remain the land of the free and the home of the brave. May God bless America.

The Difference is Obvious

What confidence in your destination requires.

*These things I have written to you who believe in
the name of the Son of God, in order that you
may know that you have eternal life.*
– 1 John 5:13

Years ago, I needed to change planes in Atlanta. Due to bad weather, I missed my connecting flight, and the best they could do was put me on the standby list with a bunch of other people. If this ever happens to you, look around the waiting area and you will quickly figure out who is on standby and who already has a ticket.

Those on standby are on edge – restless and anxious for any encouraging word from the attendant at the desk. But those who have their tickets are talking, reading magazines, totally relaxed. You see, that is the way it is when you are confident of your ultimate destination and you know that you know that you're going to Heaven. You are at peace, and you can deal with the mountain tops and the valleys in life. Jesus does not want us to live with uncertainty. He wants us to be sure of our salvation, to be confident of eternity with Him and confident – in short – that we have our ticket to Heaven. You are ready to live, really live, because you are ready to die.

Are You the Real Deal?

**The difference between genuine and
counterfeit Christianity is a "bowed head."**

*Then the righteous will shine forth as
the sun in the Kingdom of the Father.*
– Matthew 13:43a

In the parable of the wheat and the tares, a man sows wheat in his
field. That very night, an enemy comes to his field and sows tares,
which is counterfeit wheat. Wheat and tares are almost identical
until harvest time nears, when the head of the wheat, heavy with
grain, bows downward, and the fruitless tares remain straight
and tall.

How can we tell whether we are wheat or tares in God's field –
whether we are the real deal or fake? First, we must ask, "Is Jesus
ruling and reigning as King in my life?" "Is my life bowed before
God, heavy with the fruit He planted for me to bear in His name?"
If we can answer "Yes," then at the time of harvest, Jesus says we
will shine forth as the sun in the Kingdom of our Heavenly Father.

The Crown of Creation

**Man is a creature of great worth,
made a little lower than the angels.**

*What is man that You are mindful of him, and the son
of man that You visit him? For You have made him a
little lower than the angels, and You have crowned
him with glory and honor!*
– Psalm 8:4-5

Walt Whitman wrote a poem in which he expressed the desire to live among the animals. He thought the contentment, ignorance and simplicity of their existence was appealing.

We live in a culture that devalues human beings, reducing us to animals at the top of the food chain. The Bible, however, establishes man in his proper place, as the crown of God's creation, made in His image to have dominion in this world, including over the animals.

Walt Whitman could write poems about animals all day long, but no animal could ever write a poem about him. Man is far above all earthly creatures and just a little lower than the heavenly beings. Yes, God is mindful of us because we are of great worth to Him. He paid an extreme price for us.

Signs of Growth

**These three steps are essential
for a life of obedience.**

*Also, keep back thy servant from presumptuous sins;
Let them not rule over me; Then I shall be blameless,
and I shall be acquitted of great transgression.
– Psalm 19:13*

If you are aware of sin in your life, don't just say, "I'm going to do better." That is not how you handle sin. Here are three steps to take as you seek to handle sin and to be obedient to the principles of God. The first thing to do is to starve it out. Don't feed it with what you read, what you see, or where you go. Next, you cut it out. Just as you cut out weeds in a garden, you get in there and you cut out the sin in your life. And finally, you crowd it out. You fill your life with good people, good things, wholesome activities, and good thoughts. You starve it out, cut it out, and crowd it out.

Before long, your "oughts" and your "wants" will become identical, and you will experience the Holy Spirit operating in your life and confirming that you are growing in your relationship with your Heavenly Father.

Just Relax

The sooner you learn this lesson, the better!

Take My yoke upon you, and learn from Me,
for I am gentle and humble in heart, and you
shall find rest for your souls.
– Matthew 11:29

You can be yoked up with Jesus and still try to live on the basis of the flesh. Jesus said, "Take My yoke upon you." What is a yoke? It is just a piece of wood that the ox puts his head through, and another ox puts his head through. Then the one in charge leads them down the row. If a young ox gets in there and tries to pull this way and that, or goes too fast or too slow, that yoke just burns his neck and back and it is anything but light. When we get yoked up with Jesus, if we try to operate in the flesh the way we always did, and try to go our own way, we will be miserable.

Jesus says, "Just relax." And then His yoke becomes easy. When He takes the lead, He is right there with us. And He moves us right up the row – right up the path – and leads us the way we should go. His yoke, when we let Him take the lead, is easy – and His burden is light.

The Best Things in Life

Only God knows how to give the very best.

Thou will make known to me the path of life;
In Thy presence is fullness of joy;
in Thy right hand there are pleasures forever.
– Psalm 16:11

Years ago, I read a magazine article entitled, "The Best Things in Life Aren't Things." In it, the writer listed 35 things to illustrate her point – things like coming home, and the smell of freshly baked bread. If you surveyed any group of people and asked them to name the best thing in life, most would respond, "happiness." But the problem with happiness is that it is based on circumstances. Instead, I propose that the best thing in life is joy. Joy is not only God-given; it is independent of what's going on in your life. God gives us joy when we receive His son Jesus as Lord and Savior. God gave His best that we might experience the best of all gifts – His unspeakable joy.

What is My Shepherd doing?

**Like a shepherd, God has to do things
for our good that can appear harsh.**

*For momentary, light affliction is producing for us an
eternal weight of glory far beyond all comparison...
– 2 Corinthians 4:17*

While visiting a sheep ranch in Northern Wales, Christian author
Elisabeth Elliott watched shepherds placing their sheep into
vats filled with an antiseptic solution to kill deadly parasites and
insects. The process required submerging the sheep several times.
As you might expect, the fearful sheep resisted, desperately trying
to escape the vats. Elisabeth shares that she wondered if the
sheep were thinking, "Is my shepherd, who has always cared for
me, now trying to kill me?"

We can identify with those sheep. Sometimes it may seem as if our
Good Shepherd is trying to kill us, when He's really trying to heal
us and save us. Like the sheep, we wonder, "How can this possibly
be for my good?" But we can learn to trust and surrender to the
plan of a God who loves us and works things together for our good.

A Fitting Name

God's name is majestic because He is.

O Lord, our Lord, how majestic is
Your name in all the earth, Who have displayed
Your splendor above the heavens!
– Psalm 8:1

David penned these words of praise following his victory in God's name over the Philistine giant Goliath. No doubt God's name was majestic in Israel on that day. But what about today? Is the Lord's name excellent over the entire earth? There are atheists and agnostics who would answer with a resounding "No!"

Sadly, to some people, even those who go by the name of Christian, God's name is reduced to their favorite profanity or vain expression. If they would only take the time to do what David did in this Psalm – consider the work of God's fingers and the depth of His love – they would join him and millions of people in declaring, "O Lord, our Lord, how majestic is Your name in all the earth!"

It's Worth It

A right relationship with God has sweet results

And this I pray, that your love may abound still more and more in real knowledge and all discernment...having been filled with the fruit of righteousness which comes through Jesus Christ, to the glory and praise of God.
— Philippians 1:9, 11

In Hawaii, they serve a juice called POG. It's a mixture of pineapple juice, orange juice, and guava. They squeeze these three fruits together – and the result is delicious. When we begin to make excellent choices, and we have the love of Christ within us, what comes out of our life, the juice of our life, is the fruit of the Spirit that Paul writes about in Galatians. Your life will exhibit love, joy, peace, patience, kindness, and so much more.

Whatever you're going through, and in spite of the stress of circumstances – you can be confident that what God is producing in your life is worthwhile. Depend on Him, be patient with the process, and you will say, "the juice is worth the squeeze."

Holy, Holy, Holy

**Be careful not to overlook
this aspect of God's character.**

*And one called out to another and said, "Holy, Holy, Holy
is the Lord of hosts, the whole earth is full of His glory."
– Isaiah 6:3*

One of my favorite chapters in the Old Testament is Isaiah 6, which describes the prophet Isaiah's vision of the Lord on the throne of the universe. Angels are hovering around the throne and each angel has six wings. With two they covered their feet, and with two they flew. What did they do with the other two wings? They covered their faces. Even angels cannot look upon the form and the face of Almighty God.

When Isaiah saw that vision of the Lord, he cried out that he was a man with unclean lips. In the presence of God, everything that has been hidden is brought into the light. Too often we forget the true awesomeness of God. We need to take time to meditate on the holiness of God, and the radiance of God, and the omnipotence of God. Then we should pause and thank Him for the wonder that is ours – that because of the shed blood of His Son, Jesus – we can draw near, with confidence, to the very throne of grace.

People Matter to God

**This practice is the key to success
when you share your faith.**

*And they spoke the word of the Lord to him
together with all who were in his house.
— Acts 16:32*

In Acts 16, the Apostle Paul conducts a clinic on how to share your faith. I believe all Christians need to share their faith, but we each have our own style based on our giftedness and our personality. Some have an invitational style of asking people to church. Others may have a more direct, confrontational style. And still others have an intellectual style or a quieter, more philosophical approach.

But there is one aspect of personal evangelism we must never forget, and that is to listen. Find out where people are, what they believe, how they think. Ask questions, then listen, and be patient. After you have listened for a while, there will be that strategic moment when they begin to ask you what you think. Then you will have a chance to let them know that they need the Lord and let them know that they matter to God. And you may be able to love that person all the way to Jesus. People matter to God, all people, and people need the Lord. God will use you, wherever He has placed you, to share His truth with the least and the last and the lost.

Where do You Live?

Our address as believers is "in Christ."

Lord, You have been our dwelling place in all generations.
— Psalm 90:1

One of the first things parents teach their children to memorize is their home address and phone number. But knowing the answer to the question "Where do you live?" is helpful for adults, too.

Psalm 90 was written by Moses. At the end of his life, his residence was not in a place. He did not dwell in Canaan. His residence was in the Lord. God was His dwelling place. The problem with many Christians is that we do not dwell or abide in Christ. We just come for a visit on special days or in times of crisis. Jesus said, "Abide in me." We don't need to wonder for a moment where we should live. We need to make our home "in Christ," and make sure we memorize that address.

Number Your Days

**Only what we do for God in Christ
will stand the test of time.**

*So teach us to number our days, that
we may present to You a heart of wisdom.
– Psalm 90:12*

Recently, I was talking with a man who is at church whenever the doors are open. He told me he had been away from the Lord for sixty-four years, and now that he has found Christ, he wants as much of Him as he can possibly get. You might say he's making up for lost time, for the years that passed without salvation, peace, and fullness.

We learn from the prayer of Moses in Psalm 90 that we are to number, or measure, our days so we can present to God a heart of wisdom and a life of meaning. How are you at numbering your days? Do you focus on eternal things as much or even more than the things of this world? Remember, only what we do for God in Christ will stand the test of time.

Fully Human

**We can trust that God understands
everything about us.**

*After this, Jesus, knowing that all things had
already been accomplished, in order that the
Scripture might be fulfilled, said "I am thirsty."*
– John 19:28

Jesus made seven statements from the Cross which give us
a greater understanding of the very heart of our Savior. The
gospel of John records the fifth word from the Cross when
Jesus declared, "I thirst." It is not surprising that He was thirsty
after enduring several hours of beating, after carrying the cross
and being nailed to it, and after losing a great deal of blood.
Jesus was fully God and fully man, and here we see His humanity.
We see someone whose suffering was real and intense.

This word reminds us that we can never say that God doesn't
understand us. He experienced thirst, He suffered, He was tempt-
ed, and He identifies totally with us. I am so thankful that Almighty
God loves us in this fashion. Jesus accepted the sour wine offered
to him, so that He – with a swollen tongue and bleeding lips –
could speak that victorious next word – "It is finished." The bridge
between God and man is complete, and that bridge is available for
all of us today.

Wayfinding

The best guidance system in the world.

Jesus said to him, "I am the way, and the truth, and the life; no one comes to the Father, but through Me."
– John 14:6

What a wonderful word picture Jesus has given us in this verse. One day I was in one of those giant superstores, and I needed to find something. When I asked a clerk where it was, she said, "Follow me and I'll take you there." I told her that wasn't necessary, and to just give me the directions. But she insisted! She didn't just point out the way, she became "the way".

That's what Jesus is saying here. He is saying, "There isn't a chart you need to follow. You just get in Me, and I will get in You, and I will become the Way." He provides His children with a built-in guide and compass. Jesus Himself is the Way – and the Truth – and the Life.

Put Your Pen Away

**Christianity is more than a list
of requirements and prohibitions.**

*Behold, I have inscribed you on the palms of My hands...
– Isaiah 49:16*

We all know people who love to make lists. Generally, people make lists to organize information, or to prioritize their day, or to keep from forgetting something important. A lot of people think of Christianity as a list of things to do, and a list of things not to do. But you cannot define Christianity by what someone does or does not do. I could write down everything I think a Christian should not do, and it would be a pretty long list. Then I could write down what I think a Christian should do. Add those two lists together, and that is what some people think it means to be a Christian.

The accurate answer is that to be a Christian is to be right with God. It is being, not doing. We confess our sins, we turn from all known sin, we invite Jesus to come into our life, and then we are right with God. God looks at you and says, "This person is right with Me." And He writes your name on the palm of His hand where it can never be forgotten.

Perfected Power

The "ordinary" is God's natural avenue for glory.

*And He said to me, "My grace is sufficient for you,
for power is perfected in weakness." Most gladly,
therefore, I will rather boast about my weaknesses,
so that the power of Christ may dwell in me.*
– 2 Corinthians 12:9

Is it possible for God to be glorified through everyday people like you and me? The answer is absolutely yes. In fact, the "ordinary" is God's natural avenue for glory. In our scripture, Paul says that when we are weak, God is strong.

This has been God's way throughout history. Moses, a discarded baby in the bulrushes, eventually overthrew Pharaoh and his kingdom. God Himself became a baby in Bethlehem and turned our world "right side up" with His coming. The limitations of His people are a perfect backdrop to display His brilliance.

I have a friend in the diamond business. Whenever he shows a diamond, he places it on a piece of dark velvet. The dark cloth sets off the diamond beautifully. Can God's majesty and glory shine in our dark world through us? Yes, it can, and it does, and it will.

Even Greater

God's challenges are custom made just for us.

*Truly, truly, I say to you, he who believes in Me,
the works that I do shall he do also; and greater works
than these shall he do; because I go to the Father.*
– John 14:12

A large, muscular mountain man encountered a much smaller
man. The smaller man said, "If I was as big as you, I'd go out in
the woods, find the biggest bear I could, and I'd throw him to the
ground." But the larger man replied, "If I were you, I'd go out there
and find a little bear, and I'd pick him up and fling him to
the ground."

That's our problem, isn't it? We focus too much on what others
are doing rather than trusting God to provide what we need to
accomplish the tasks He has prepared for us. So often we say, "If
only I had his resources, or her education, or their opportunities."
Instead, we need to trust that God will provide what we need to
accomplish those works that He has custom made just for you –
and just for me.

At Home

The most beautiful word for Heaven.

In My Father's house are many dwelling places;
if it were not so, I would have told you;
for I go to prepare a place for you.
– John 14:2

What is Jesus saying in this verse? Simply that His children will spend all of eternity with Him in the Father's house. There are a lot of names in the New Testament for Heaven. Heaven is called a Kingdom because it has principles upon which it will operate. It is called a country because it is vast. It is called a city because it has a large population. And it is also called Paradise, because it is beautiful beyond comprehension. But the best word for Heaven, I think, is "My Father's house."

When we get to Heaven, we will realize we never truly felt at home on Earth. But, in Heaven, we will discover that, in the Father's house, we feel "right at home."

Abundance

God gives more than we ask or expect.

*Now to Him who is able to do exceeding abundantly
beyond all that we ask or think, according
to the power that works within us...*
– Ephesians 3:20-21

When you ask God to help you carry out a task He has given you, you can be sure you will receive more than you requested. God gives us more opportunity, and more provisions, and more success than we could ever imagine.

It's like the story of two hunters who were offered $100 for every wolf they could capture and deliver alive. One night, when they were way up in the mountains, they awoke to discover they were surrounded by 50 wolves with glaring eyes and bared teeth. While the first hunter was terrified, the second one just punched him and said, "Look, we've struck it rich!" Ask God to help you use your gifts, talents and abilities for Him, and you'll be overwhelmed by the result. You'll think you've struck it rich!

"I Can't See Jesus"

Jesus towers above all else in this world!

Therefore, since we have so great a cloud of witnesses surrounding us, let us also lay aside every encumbrance and the sin which so easily entangles us, and let us run with endurance the race that is set before us, fixing our eyes on Jesus, the author and perfecter of faith, who for the joy set before Him endured the cross, despising the shame, and has sat down at the right hand of the throne of God.
– Hebrews 12:1-2

A small country church had a portrait of Jesus behind its pulpit. One Sunday the church had a guest speaker who was considerably taller than the pastor. While he was speaking, a little girl on the front row looked at her mother and whispered, "Where's the man who usually talks? This one is too big. I can't see Jesus."

What keeps us from seeing Jesus? Our scripture states that the burdens of life and the sins that trip us up can become so over-whelming they can hide Jesus. So what can we do? Exactly what our scripture urges us to do. We must keep our eyes fixed on Jesus. His love demonstrated on the Cross and His power revealed in the resurrection and ascension tower above everything and everyone we encounter in this world. With such an attitude of faith, nothing can hide Jesus from our sight.

The Holy Spirit Is a S.T.U.D.

**The Holy Spirit is our support in spiritual growth,
both vertically and horizontally.**

*But the Helper, the Holy Spirit, whom the Father will
send in My name, He will teach you all things,
and bring to your remembrance all that I said to you.
– John 14:26*

We can study and understand the ethics of Socrates without ever knowing Socrates. But we cannot understand the Bible and spiritual truth without knowing Jesus Christ and having the Holy Spirit teach us. The Holy Spirit is like the studs in a building that provide vertical and horizontal support. We can use STUD as an acrostic to see some of the ways He operates in our lives.

"The Holy Spirit searches our spirits in truth. He teaches us all things, even the thoughts of God. Also, the Holy Spirit gives us understanding of the truth of God's Word, leading to a discernment of the will and purpose of God in our lives and circumstances." So let me encourage you to do an inspection of your life in Christ and pay special attention to the studs.

The Man Behind the Curtain

God's wisdom leads to life that is alive with purpose, meaning, and power.

I was with you in weakness and in fear and in much trembling, and my message and my preaching were not in persuasive words of wisdom, but in demonstration of the Spirit and of power, so that your faith would not rest on the wisdom of men, but on the power of God.
– 1 Corinthians 2:3-5

Most of us have seen the classic children's movie *The Wizard of Oz*, with Dorothy skipping down the yellow brick road to see the great and powerful Oz and asking him to help her get home to Kansas. Ultimately, we discover the Wizard of Oz is a phony when Dorothy's dog, Toto, pulls back a curtain revealing a mere human with a loud microphone.

The film provides a fitting depiction of human wisdom, as Dorothy discovers she had everything she needed all along to get home. No greater help was necessary. Human wisdom, however, never brings true joy, meaning, or fulfillment. But God's wisdom leads to a life that is alive with purpose, meaning, and power: a life of abundance. We know that to be true because, when we pull back that curtain, we discover we have a "Greater Help" that is essential for life: the power of God through Jesus Christ.

The Sticking Point

**The resurrection of Jesus Christ is the most
established event in antiquity.**

*Why do you seek the living One among the dead?
He is not here, but He has risen. Remember how He
spoke to you while He was still in Galilee, saying that
the Son of Man must be delivered into the hands of
sinful men, and be crucified, and the third day rise again.*
– Luke 24:5b-7

One of the world's largest container ships was stuck in the Suez
Canal, halting global trade for six days at a cost of nine billion dollars per day. Like that ship, many people get stuck on the resurrection of Jesus Christ. Born at Christmas? Okay. Died on the cross
for our sins? Okay. Rose from the dead? Stuck. They can't get
past it. But thanks to historical forensic evidence and hundreds of
eyewitness accounts, this "sticking point" is the most established
event in antiquity.

The resurrection of Jesus Christ validates all of His claims, His
teachings, His miracles, His very life as recorded in the proven
truth of God's Word. Therefore, because Christ has risen, those
of us in Him have the assurance that we too shall rise and spend
eternity with Him, which leaves me with only one more word:
Hallelujah!

Ghost Forest

**The church and believers must guard its foundation
against the penetration of a poisonous culture.**

*And do not be conformed to this world, but be
transformed by the renewing of your mind so that
you may prove what the will of God is, that which
is good and acceptable and perfect.*
– Romans 12:2

There are more varieties of trees in North Carolina than in any other state. During the three months of fall, over five million people provide over a billion dollars of income to the state, as they come to enjoy the kaleidoscope of color in the trees. But in 2011, Hurricane Irene sent saltwater deeper inland than ever before, killing over twenty-one thousand acres of trees, creating a ghost forest. Like that saltwater, a secular culture can poison the roots, or the foundation, of a nation, church, or life. And when the foundation is destroyed, nothing stands.

How can we protect ourselves from the saltwater of secular culture? According to our verse, we pull out our "transformers" – our Bibles – and spend time daily renewing our minds. This exercise will not only keep us from conforming to culture, it will also equip us to "reverse the flow" and penetrate culture with the pure and living water of Jesus Christ.

A Warm Welcome

Returning to the Lord is the key to experiencing His blessing.

*"Therefore say to them, Thus says the Lord of hosts,
"Return to Me," declares the Lord of hosts,
"that I may return to you, "says the Lord of hosts..."
– Zechariah 1:3*

A writer named David Redding wrote about growing up on a farm in Scotland. As a young boy, he was given a beautiful black puppy he named Teddy. Redding and Teddy were inseparable. When Redding had to go to war, he was unable to return home for more than two years. But even so, when he got a half mile from the family farm, he heard Teddy barking. Redding said he just whistled, and Teddy recognized that whistle and came bounding toward him. Redding observed, "If a dog can receive me back after I've been away for such a long time, how much more will God welcome and receive me when I return to Him."

Whether you have wandered off, run off, or gotten so caught up in the agenda of the world that you have gradually drifted away from God, this story is a reminder that you will be welcome when you return to the Father.

A Love Blockage

Heartaches can release love through new and different channels.

Beloved, let us love one another, for love is from God; and everyone who loves is born of God and knows God. The one who does not love does not know God, for God is love.
– 1 John 4:7-8

Corrie Ten Boom was a Dutch Christian whose family helped hide the Jews during Hitler's regime in World War II. There is a movie about her life called *The Hiding Place.* When she was younger, Corrie loved a young man she believed would become her husband. Instead, he married her best friend. Heartbroken, she received consolation from her dad. "Corrie, you are a victim of blocked love. You can take that love and keep it locked up and become bitter, or you can release that love and shower it on others." She chose to release her love in Jesus' name and to have a ministry that would impact millions.

Is there a love blockage in your life? Don't become bitter and miserable. Remove the blockage, so you too can love and serve others in Jesus' name.

Partial Obedience

Partial obedience is actually disobedience.

*Samuel said, "Has the Lord as much delight
in burnt offerings and sacrifices as in obeying the
voice of the Lord? Behold, to obey is better than
sacrifice, and to heed than the fat of rams."
– 1 Samuel 15:22*

Partial obedience is disobedience, and it cost Saul his reign as Israel's king. God had instructed him to destroy the wicked Amalekites. Instead, Saul stopped short of completing his assignment, even taking as spoils from battle the choicest of goods and livestock. When confronted by God's prophet Samuel, Saul offered the dubious rationalization that he spared the animals to use as a sacrifice to God. Samuel rebuked Saul, saying, "Behold, to obey is better than sacrifice."

Obedience matters to God. In fact, Jesus said that we prove our love for Him by obeying His commandments. Are there areas of disobedience in your life? If so, confess them to God, receive His forgiveness through the sacrifice of Christ, and begin a life of obedience today.

God's Magnificent Design

God reveals Himself in the beauty of the world He created.

The heavens are telling of the glory of God; and the firmament is declaring the work of His hands.
— Psalm 19:1

Noted author H. G. Wells once said that, when he was young, he would look into the starry skies and he would be overwhelmed by the mystery and the majesty of creation. It would take his breath away. But, in an interview he gave when he was an old man, he said that all the mystery was gone, all the glory was gone. He said, "I look into the heavens just like I would look at wallpaper in a waiting room." How sad that is!

If we aren't careful, the jadedness of life can take away the grandeur of God's created order. Never lose sight of the wonder that this world was designed by God - and that we are a part of His magnificent design. That knowledge will help your life catch fire, it will renew your passion – and it will cause you to declare the glory of God.

Out of the Cage

What appears to restrain us may really be for our protection.

*Now the Lord is the Spirit; and where the
Spirit of the Lord is, there is liberty.*
– 2 Corinthians 3:17

One summer Bob Bartlett, a wonderful explorer, filled a boat with rare birds, put them in cages, and began to transport them to America. Somewhere in the Atlantic, the boat encountered rough water, and one of the birds got away. They watched the bird fly away to apparent "freedom." But, several hours later, the bird came back. He couldn't find any land, so he returned to the ship.

What had once been a prison was now the only way this bird could get across the ocean. We can be confident that Jesus, as our Savior, is our Rock and our strength, and that following Him is the only certain path to freedom. We need to pray, "Make me a captive, Lord, so that I can be truly free."

What Does God Look Like?

In Christ we see the true image of God!

He is the image of the invisible God,
the firstborn of all creation.
– Colossians 1:15

On a visit to the Vatican's Sistine Chapel, I spent time studying the famous frescoes of Michelangelo on its ceiling, particularly God's creation of man. As I looked at the figure of God reaching down toward Adam, it occurred to me that Creator God merely looked like an "older Adam."

We tend to make God look like us. But God is not a man. God is spirit. So how can we know what He looks like and what His image should look like in us? God answered that question when He clothed Himself in human flesh, demonstrating the dignity He sees in man and in His Son, Jesus Christ. Yes, God became man, and in Jesus we see the true, full image of God Almighty, the image He wants others to see in us.

Open Door Opportunities

It really is true: when God closes a door, He opens another one.

At the same time, pray also for us, that God may open for us a door for the word, to declare the mystery of Christ...
– Colossians 4:3

Fanny Crosby was one of the most prolific hymnists in history. Although blind from infancy, she composed thousands of songs and poems, became a teacher, and worked in rescue missions. While some may have regarded her blindness as a closed door in her life, Fanny used her blindness as an opportunity to share the Word of God.

Do you feel like God has closed a door in your life? It may or may not be a physical infirmity like Fanny's. It may be in your vocation, or in a relationship, or even in your life's dream. Whatever the situation, your closed door is actually God's "open door opportunity" for you to share His Word and to declare the life-changing truth of Jesus Christ.

Faith is the Victory

The victory is won long before the battle takes place.

But you, when you pray, go into your inner room,
close your door and pray to your Father
who is in secret, and your Father who sees
what is done in secret will reward you.
– Matthew 6:6

When you watch a championship football team, you might say, "Boy, they won that game today!" But they didn't. They won that game long before through training, through discipline, and through all that went into their preparation. That is the same with us.

The faith to live for God, in victory, comes day by day, week by week, year by year, in the secret places where we learn to trust and obey. It is in the secret place that we seek God, and He begins to lead us and empower us. That is where we learn to trust and obey, so that we can be victorious in the public arena.

The ability to trust – and to obey – is learned and refined when no one is around, when no one notices, and when no one applauds.

The Ultimate Source

The armor of God will help you stand firm in battle.

Finally, be strong in the Lord,
and in the strength of His might.
– Ephesians 6:10

We are all familiar with the account of David and Goliath. Remember how, when David went out to fight the giant, King Saul insisted that David put on his royal armor. Initially, David tried putting on Saul's armor and sword. But he was uncomfortable in them, and so he told the king, "I cannot go with these, for I have not tested them."

This account gives us an important principle. Don't try to fight your battles in someone else's armor. That's the point. You are unique. God created you by prescription, and He has a plan for what you are to become by His grace.

Don't try to imitate someone else. David was wise enough to say, "I can't fight in this armor." In the battles you will face in this life, don't trust any armor other than the armor of God.

First Fruits

First fruits of the Spirit are a foretaste of what we will become in Christ.

And not only this, but also we ourselves, having the first fruits of the Spirit,...groan within ourselves, waiting eagerly for our adoption...the redemption of our body.
– Romans 8:23

First fruits are the preview of an entire crop. For example, if you grow corn and the first ears harvested are delicious, then you know you have an outstanding crop of corn. The presence of the Holy Spirit in our lives is the foretaste – the first fruits – of all that we will someday become. Until then, our present existence is similar to the pains of labor before birth.

Do parents offer to show pictures of the labor and delivery process? Of course not. But they are quick to show pictures of their beautiful new baby. So as we groan now, having these first fruits of the Spirit, we are looking forward to seeing the picture of our resurrected life with Christ in glory. Are the first fruits of God's Spirit evident in your life?

The Christian's Placard

The message of Jesus Christ crucified must be carried to all people.

And when I came to you, brethren, I did not come with superiority of speech or of wisdom, proclaiming to you the testimony of God. For I determined to know nothing among you except Jesus Christ, and Him crucified.
– 1 Corinthians 2: 1-2

Before mass printing was available, important information was often communicated by people carrying placards which would contain only essential words and information. Today, advertisers still use placard carriers, many of them spinning their signs on street corners and other public places in order to catch our attention. In our scripture, we see the words that formed the core of every message the Apostle Paul delivered: "Jesus Christ crucified." You might say these words were his placard.

The message of Jesus Christ crucified should be the placard every believer carries, with urgency. For it is at the cross of Jesus that God demonstrates how much He loves us, and how much He wants us to come home to Him. Pick up and carry the Christian's placard with you everywhere you go, and do whatever you can to draw attention to its life-changing message: Jesus Christ crucified.

No Necktie, No Service

We can miss God's answers to our prayers.

*And whatever you ask in My name, that I will do,
that the Father may be glorified in the Son.
– John 14:13*

A man lost in the desert spotted an approaching traveler. "Please," he begged, "give me some water." The traveler replied, "I don't have any water, but I will give you my necktie." "What? I don't need a necktie, I need water!" So the thirsty man staggered away. He soon came upon a restaurant and entered. "Finally," he thought, "I will get water!" However, the maître d' stopped him. "Sorry sir, but we can't let you in without a necktie."

Sometimes we don't believe our prayers have been answered, when actually we have rejected God's true answer. God loves us so much, He gives us exactly what we need, not what we may want at that moment. So if you're ever in the desert and a man offers you a necktie, take it, and say, "Thank you!" It just may be God's answer to your prayer.

Say What?

God's language of love needs no interpreter.

This is how God showed his love among us:
He sent his one and only Son into the world that we
might live through him. This is love: not that we
loved God, but that he loved us and sent his
Son as an atoning sacrifice for our sins.
– 1 John 4:9-10

Every profession has its own specialized language, or way of communicating its purpose and intentions. I have a friend who is an NFL quarterback. He recently shared with me one of the plays he called in the huddle. It was as if he were speaking a foreign language! The play call was a compilation of letters, numbers, adjectives, directions, and words that seemed nonsensical. I thought I knew football, but I had to ask him to interpret this play for me.

God's language, however, needs no interpreter. It can be understood by all people because God speaks the language of love. He not only speaks His language through His Word, the Bible, He also demonstrates it for all to see; for it is at the Cross of Christ that God communicates "loud and clear" His language of love to the world!

A Holy Sigh

Jesus understands our infirmities and has compassion on us, and He seeks to restore us to the image of God.

Jesus took him aside from the crowd, by himself, and put His fingers into his ears, and after spitting, He touched his tongue with the saliva; and looking up to heaven with a deep sigh, He said to him, "Ephphatha!" that is, "Be opened!"
— Mark 7:33-34

Some friends brought a man to Jesus who could not hear or speak clearly, and they entreated Jesus to heal him. They probably expected Jesus to simply touch him, or speak to him, and they were no doubt surprised at what Jesus did. I especially want you to notice something we might easily overlook in this passage. It says that Jesus looked up to Heaven with a deep sigh. I don't usually think about Divinity sighing, do you? Why did Jesus sigh? Was He saying, "This is not the way it is supposed to be"? He knew that illness and infirmity are often the result of evil in this world.

I believe that when Jesus sighed, He did so in frustration and tears, and it was a holy sigh. I wonder, as God looks at you and looks at me, when He sees what we are in comparison to what He intended for us to be, does He sigh?

Five Stones

God promises to reward the humble.

For the Lord takes delight in his people;
he crowns the humble with victory.
– Psalm 149:4

Why did David, who was skilled with a sling, pick up five stones when he went out to fight Goliath? Some have speculated that it was because Goliath had brothers, but I don't think that is the reason. I think those five stones represented something no one except God would observe. You know what it was? Humility.

Humility is when you are a champion, but you know that without God that is all you are. David said, "The victory belongs to God." He knew where his strength came from, and he wanted God to get all the glory. Those five stones indicated David's commitment to walk humbly with His God. And that, we know from His Word, is what delights our Heavenly Father.

God's Smoke Detector

How to keep God at the center of your life.

And which of you by being anxious
can add a single cubit to his life's span?
– Luke 12:25

Anxiety is like smoke. When anxiety comes into your life, follow it to its source in the way you look for the source of smoke. Anxiety comes when we take something that is good, and we put that in the place of God. We take a good gift from God – our vocation, our children, a hobby – and we make that the thing that we look to for happiness or fulfillment. When that good thing we've put in the place of God is in jeopardy or is removed from our life, it makes us anxious.

So, any time you have anxiety, follow the smoke. More than likely, you will find the source is that which caused you to move God out of the center of your life and put some "good thing" there instead.

Road Signs

God's Word provides a reliable early warning system.

But examine everything carefully; hold fast to that which is good; abstain from every form of evil.
– 1 Thessalonians 5:21-22

Imagine a high mountain road with dangerous curves and rocks. The highway department can do one of two things. They can put a hospital at the bottom of the mountain where they can treat people who have wrecks on the road. Or they can put up signs along the dangerous passage, such as "slow down," or "watch for falling rocks," or "sharp curve ahead." And hopefully people will heed these warnings and avoid an accident.

God has put up warning signs throughout the Bible. Because He loves us, God will minister to us with His grace when we crash because we ignored the signs. But how much better to heed the signs that say "No" or "Stop" or "Dead End Street." We can find these signs all through the Bible – from the 10 Commandments all the way to the admonitions in Revelation.

Out on a Limb

God always takes the initiative in seeking and saving us.

So he ran on ahead and climbed up into a sycamore tree in order to see Him, for He was about to pass through that way. When Jesus came to the place, He looked up and said to him, "Zaccheus, hurry and come down, for today I must stay at your house."
– Luke 19:4-5

The familiar story of Zaccheus, the tax collector, is a beautiful picture of how we get into a relationship with God in Jesus Christ. It starts when we are willing to climb out on a limb and admit that we want Jesus to change the way we think, the way we live, to forgive us, and to clean up our lives. We get in the proximity of Jesus. Then, He does the seeking. He does the saving.

We think we've searched for God. Oh no - He was already there before you arrived. But when you crawl out on that limb, He will go home with you and make you into the person He has equipped you to be.

Show Me

How to demonstrate that you truly love God.

*And a second is like it, "You shall
love your neighbor as yourself."*
– Matthew 22:39

One day someone went to Jesus and asked, "What is the number one commandment?" Jesus replied, "You shall love the Lord your God with all your heart, and with all your soul, and with all your mind." The crowd probably would have said, "Good answer!" Every Jewish boy would have answered the question in the same way. But then Jesus added a second commandment. He said we are to love our neighbors as we love ourselves.

The first one is rather abstract, rather intangible. It is easy to say, "Oh, I love God." But the second brings it down into the concrete and says we are to love our neighbor as we love ourselves. So, if you say you love God, the genuineness of that love is demonstrated by how you love others. That makes all the difference, doesn't it?

Put Up Your Flag

How to align your profession with your conduct.

*For this reason we must pay much closer attention
to what we have heard, lest we drift away from it.
– Hebrews 2:1*

After a passenger train was struck by an oncoming freight train, the engineer was asked whether he had seen the flagman who was trying to get the train to stop. The engineer replied, "Yes, I saw the flag, but it wasn't the red flag that indicates danger, but a yellow flag which simply means to slow down." Upon examination, it became apparent that the once-red flag had faded to a dull yellow and had lost its color and meaning.

That can happen to us if we get caught up in things that distract us from our commitment to Christ. Once you put up your flag for Christ, that means you are available to serve Him, to worship Him, to study His Word, and that you never lose sight of God's desire to make your life extraordinary.

Three Big Things

An encounter with Jesus will transform any life.

For this reason I say to you, her sins, which
are many, have been forgiven, for she loved much,
but he who is forgiven little, loves little.
– Luke 7:47

What did this woman, this "sinner" as Luke describes her, who anointed the feet of Jesus with perfume, receive in return? She got three big things that every one of us would desire to have in our own life.

First, she received the capacity to love, because she realized the depth of her sin and how completely and how deeply she had experienced forgiveness. Second, she received joy. The burden and the guilt of her sin had been lifted and she had been set free. And third, she received peace. Literally, Jesus said to her, "Your faith has saved you; go in peace." The rest of her life would be an adventure of peace. Love! Joy! Peace! Who would not want those three big things?

At His Feet

All you need to handle a crisis.

There is no one holy like the Lord; indeed, there is no one besides You, nor is there any rock like our God.
– 1 Samuel 2:2

How do you handle a challenge, whether it is a simple molehill kind of problem or a Mount Everest moment where the whole of life has bottomed out? First, slow down, and remember that God has said that we are to cease striving and know that He is God (Psalm 46:10). Next, take a time out to get your priorities right, and recall that our number one priority is to seek His kingdom (Matthew 7:33).

Finally, focus on the big picture. Ask God to help you see the situation from the perspective of eternity by bringing Christ into the equation. Does that sound daunting? How can we keep all these things in our resources for living? The answer: Worship. Sit at the feet of Jesus, submit to His Word, listen for His voice, and worship Him. That's where and how we can effectively handle the challenges of life.

Prepare the Way

Repentance prepares the way for Christ to enter a heart.

For of His fullness we have all received,
and grace upon grace.
— John 1:16

While visiting the historic settlement at Williamsburg, Virginia, I noticed several groundskeepers carefully combing the gravel paths and removing any rough stones. I asked one of them if they did that every day. He replied, "No, but we're expecting the Emperor of Japan this week, so we're making sure all the pathways are level and straight."

That is what John the Baptist did as he prepared the way for Jesus Christ as the coming Messiah. How did he do it? By being a voice in the wilderness with the message "Repent! Turn from your sin!" It is repentance that prepares the way for Jesus, our King, to enter our hearts. Have you prepared the way for the Lord by turning from your sin? If not, start combing the gravel and removing the rough stones.

Hi Dad! Bye Dad!

**Fathers are to model the love, provision,
and protection of God, the Heavenly Father.**

*Fathers, do not exasperate your children,
so that they will not lose heart.
– Colossians 3:21*

A child in our church was asked, "If there were a TV show about your family, what would it be called?" The youngster answered, "Hi Dad! Bye Dad!" His reply spoke volumes about his longing for the love and attention of his "workaholic" dad. Fatherhood is a relationship. So any man who is not involved in the lives of his children and is clueless to their struggles, dreams, and desires is not really a father.

Without a doubt, our earthly dads impact our concept of God, our Heavenly Father. Sadly, though, many dads make it difficult for their children to believe there really is a Father in Heaven who loves them and desires a relationship with them. So, dads, what idea of "father" are you planting in your kids?

All It Takes

How to pray in a moment of desperation

*But seeing the wind, he became frightened, and when
he began to sink, he cried out, saying, "Lord, save me!"
– Matthew 14:30*

I don't know if this is the shortest prayer in the Bible, but it is definitely brief! I like this prayer; it is a passionate S.O.S. Remember how the disciples saw Jesus walking to them on the Sea of Galilee, and Peter asked Jesus to command him to walk on the water to Him. Once Peter took his eyes off Jesus, he began to sink, and he didn't have time for any formal or fancy language. He just cried out in desperation, "Lord, save me."

Sometimes, when difficulty comes into our lives, and we realize we need to get serious about the Lord, all we may be able to do at the moment is cry out, "Lord, save me!" But that is all it really takes. When we cry in desperation to the One Who can rescue us, we can be confident that the Lord is ready – and waiting – and will reach out His hand.

Like Father, Like Son

Our children don't do what we say; they do what we do!

*These words, which I am commanding you today,
shall be on your heart. You shall teach them diligently
to your sons and shall talk of them when you sit
in your house and when you walk by the way and
when you lie down and when you rise up.*
– Deuteronomy 6:6-7

Years ago, there was an anti-smoking commercial that showed a little boy doing everything just like his dad. It really was cute watching the little toddler copy his dad's every action, that is, until the dad sat down under a tree to smoke a cigarette. The commercial ends with the little boy picking up the pack of cigarettes and a voice saying, "Like father, like son."

That commercial served as a reminder of an important fact: our children will do as we say for a while, but eventually they will do as we do. That's why it is so important that we model genuine Christianity for our children; that our walk matches our talk.

Parents, make sure your children see your personal, loving devotion to God. Believe me, they are watching you!

A Pile of Trouble

**The trustworthy instruction from parents
and God is for our own good.**

*Children, be obedient to your parents in all things,
for this is well-pleasing to the Lord.
– Colossians 3:20*

When I was a young boy, my dad took me to look at some cattle. He warned me to stay clear of the animals because they could hurt a little guy like me. "No fun," I muttered. Then I spotted a little calf. I thought, "I'm bigger than he is. He couldn't hurt me." But as I approached it, bam! That "cute little calf" knocked me down right into a big pile of manure. I should have obeyed my dad's warning, but even at an early age, I thought I could ignore it and handle the situation on my own.

I've done that with God at times, too, and so have you. God's warnings and boundaries are not to spoil our fun but are for our protection. So trust and obey the Lord. It just may keep you out of a "pile of trouble."

Doubt Your Doubts

What we focus on influences our outlook on life.

But let him ask in faith without any doubting,
for the one who doubts is like the surf of the
sea driven and tossed by the wind.
– James 1:6

A fly on the back of an elephant won't hurt him unless the elephant panics and runs over a cliff. In a similar sense, there is nothing wrong with doubt. Doubts will come into your life and my life, but the danger only comes when we major on them, amplify them, and meditate and think about them. When that happens, pretty soon we are more focused on our doubt than on our faith. Instead, we need to get into the posture of being able to doubt our doubts. That is where faith begins to grow and becomes valid.

Are you wrestling with doubt? I have good news today. God is still on His Throne. He is in control and He will help you "doubt your doubts" and transform them into steadfast faith in Him.

Perspective

**Our hardships are God's tools of love designed
to help us grow up and grow strong.**

*No discipline seems pleasant at the time, but painful.
Later on, however, it produces a harvest of righteousness
and peace for those who have been trained by it.*
– Hebrews 12:11

The birth of a giraffe is quite an event. The mother stands during the process, so the newborn calf enters the world with a thud! Then the mother gives her newborn a hard kick to get it to stand. It usually takes several kicks before the calf can stay upright on strong legs. From our perspective, the mother giraffe's actions seem cruel. But from the perspective of life and survival, that mother knows her little giraffe has limited time to be able to stand on its own.

Likewise, from our perspective, we might wonder if God really cares about the "thuds and kicks" in our lives. But from His perspective, they are His tools of love, preparing us for spiritual survival. God's aim is that we grow up, and like that baby giraffe, when we get knocked down, we will get up stronger each time.

Why Are You Here?

We are to glorify God in the majestic and the mundane.

Whether, then, you eat or drink or whatever
you do, do all to the glory of God.
— 1 Corinthians 10:31

Mark Twain is credited with saying that the two most important days in your life are the day you are born and the day you find out why. God appointed the day of our birth, and He has appointed the day of our death. But what about the days in between? Why are we here?

We are here first and foremost to love God and glorify Him in all that we do, both the majestic and the mundane. Whether we are worshiping or working, eating or drinking, spending time in prayer or spending time with friends and family, we are to do it in a way that exalts God. So if you were made to love and glorify God, why not begin right now. It is the "why" that will make this day one of the most important days in your life.

Nicknames

This is a name you won't be ashamed to bear.

And I will be a Father to you, and you shall be sons
and daughters to Me, says the Lord Almighty.
– 2 Corinthians 6:18

I suspect many of you had a nickname when you were younger. We generally don't like our nicknames, do we? I remember a coach in junior high called me "Speedball." I didn't know what he meant by that, so I didn't like it. Later in life, we don't want people to know our nickname because we probably spent a lot of time trying to live it down.

But did you know you have a nickname that God gave you when you became a Christian? God looked at you and said, "Your nickname is 'son' or 'daughter.'" He stamped His name on your life. And now He says, "I have given this name to you. Live up to it!"

Our Purpose is God's Pleasure

**When we are in the will of God and glorifying Him,
we will feel His pleasure.**

*For this reason, since the day we heard about you,
we have not stopped praying for you. We continually
ask God to fill you with the knowledge of his will
through all the wisdom and understanding that the
Spirit gives so that you may live a life worthy of the
Lord and please him in every way: bearing fruit in
every good work, growing in the knowledge of God.
– Colossians 1:9-10*

The Academy Award winning movie *Chariots of Fire* depicts the life of Scottish Olympian and Christian missionary Eric Liddell. Some of Liddell's family and friends questioned the time he was giving to his training and running, reminding him he was called to be a missionary in China. In a scene with his sister, Liddell says, "God made me for a purpose, for China. But He also made me fast, and when I run, I feel His pleasure." Eric Liddell did not run for fun, fame, or fortune. He ran to honor God. And yes, he honored God as a missionary in China until his death.

When we know God's purpose for our lives, and we use our gifts and talents to glorify and honor Him, we too will feel His pleasure.

God is Never Late

God's timing is always perfect.

Wait for the Lord; Be strong and let your heart take courage; Yes, wait for the Lord!
– Psalm 27:14

Robert was growing bored in retirement, so he became a Walmart greeter. The customers loved his cheerful and engaging personality. But there was a problem: Robert was perpetually late for work. So the manager called him into his office. "Robert, without question you are one of our best greeters. However, you are always late. Now I know your career was in the military. What did they say when you showed up late?" Robert smiled and replied, "Well, they usually said, 'Good morning, General. May I bring you a cup of coffee?'"

Do you ever feel like God is late? You wonder if He's ever going to show up to help you. The truth is, God's timing is always perfect. Plus, our waiting on Him deepens our closeness to Him. Believe me, God will show up in the nick of time, and He's always worth the wait.

It's Complete

What more could anyone need for an abundant life?

The thief comes only to steal, and kill,
and destroy; I came that they might have life,
and might have it abundantly.
– John 10:10

What is it that we need most in life? One thing is light, and we know that Jesus said, "I am the Light of the world." We don't need to walk in darkness; we can walk in the Light. We also need air. That's the Holy Spirit, the Spirit of God flowing in and empowering those who are God's children. We must have water. Jesus said, "Drink deeply of Me. I give Living Water that satisfies as nothing else can." And we need bread, right? Jesus is the Bread of Life, and He promises that anyone who eats of this bread will live forever.

Jesus nourishes us and gives us everything we need. He offers all of these to members of His family, to those who have received Him. Jesus came to give us LIFE – and that life is an abundant life, a life that is complete in Him.

A Restored Relationship

**The tragic result of sin is not a broken rule,
but a broken relationship.**

*For there is one God, and one mediator also between
God and men, the man Christ Jesus, who gave Himself as
a ransom for all, the testimony given at the proper time.*
— 1 Timothy 2:5-6

In Genesis, we are told that Adam and Eve walked with God in
the Garden of Eden. Can you imagine the fellowship and joy they
experienced? But that all ended when they disobeyed God and ate
fruit from the forbidden tree. It is from this disobedience that we
learn an important truth: the tragic result of sin is not a broken
rule, but a broken relationship. Yet God, in His grace and mercy,
has provided a way to restore our relationship and fellowship with
Him through His Son, Jesus Christ.

The finished work of Jesus on the Cross is God's invitation to come
to Him and to know Him. It is an invitation to anyone and everyone,
and it comes with an RSVP card and stamped return envelope.
Have you replied yet?

Abandoned

True security is found in surrender to God.

But I do not consider my life of any account as
dear to myself, so that I may finish my course and
the ministry which I received from the Lord Jesus,
to testify solemnly of the gospel of the grace of God.
– Acts 20:24

One definition of the word "abandon" is to give oneself over without reservation, holding nothing back. Take for example people who jump out of airplanes or off cliffs or tall bridges. They "abandon" themselves to their parachutes and bungee cords.

In Acts chapter 20, we find the Apostle Paul saying farewell to the church in Ephesus. Although he knew hardship, persecution, and danger were in his future, he informed the believers that he was "abandoned" – totally sold out and surrendered – to God. He had placed his life into God's hands, and in this abandonment, he found security.

Are you abandoned to God and His purpose and plan for your life? I can guarantee that His hands are much more reliable than any parachute or bungee cord, and that your life experiences will be much more exciting. So abandon yourself. Sell out. Surrender. God's hands await you.

Lift Him Up

Does your life reflect the light of Christ shining through you?

He must increase, but I must decrease.
– John 3:30

Years ago, a pastor friend of mine told me about an elderly woman in his congregation. She might have been 100 years old, but she was there every Sunday and she sat right in the front of the sanctuary. Sometimes, if a visiting speaker filled his message with stories and illustrations, you would hear the woman whisper, "Lift Him up!" And if the speaker just continued in the same vein, she would get a little louder, "Lift Him up!" If the speaker did not present Jesus Christ with power, and honor, and glory, you can be sure he was in for a long day!

Ladies and gentlemen, that is our purpose too. We are to reflect the light of Christ, and in every way we can, we are to lift Him up. When we lift up the Lord Jesus Christ, great things can – and do – happen!

Jesus Breaks Down Barriers

**Jesus breaks down barriers that inhibit people
from seeing others as God sees them.**

*There is neither Jew nor Greek, there is neither
slave nor free man, there is neither male nor
female; for you are all one in Christ Jesus.*
– Galatians 3:28

Jesus breaks down barriers. Nowhere is that more evident than in
His encounter with the Samaritan woman at the well in the fourth
chapter of John's Gospel. During this one midday conversation,
Jesus broke through an intense racial and religious division
between the Jews and the Samaritans. He also broke down a
degrading cultural barrier by speaking to a woman in public. Most
of all, Jesus broke down the barrier that stands between God and
you and me: SIN. The ground is level at the foot of the Cross.

As Paul states in Galatians 3:8, we are all one, or equal, in Christ
Jesus. Because of this truth, God compels us to break down barriers with the name of Jesus on our lips and the lifestyle of Jesus
in our hearts. If we do that, we can change our families, our cities,
even our world.

God's Classroom

**We should always be ready and willing to
learn the lessons God has to teach us.**

*I will instruct you and teach you in the way which you
should go; I will counsel you with My eye upon you.
– Psalm 32:8*

My mother could get my attention just by looking at me or rolling
her eyes! In a way, that is what God does with us. First, He says
that He will instruct us. That is a classroom setting. He says, "I am
going to set you in a classroom and I am going to give you My personal instruction. Then I will teach you as you walk in the way." He
also says, "I will counsel with you." Isn't that terrific? And next He
says, "I'm going to keep my eye on you. I am going to watch after
you." It is incredible to realize that God "keeps His eye" on us and
promises to look out for us.

When David contemplated these truths – that we worship a God
who instructs us and keeps His eye on us, he ended this psalm by
declaring to all who trust in God, "Be glad in the Lord – and shout
for joy!"

God Delights in His Children

When we receive Christ, we become God's children.

*When He had been baptized, Jesus came up
immediately from the water; and behold, the heavens
were opened to Him, and He saw the Spirit of God
descending like a dove and alighting upon Him.
And suddenly a voice came from heaven, saying,
"This is My beloved Son, in whom I am well pleased."
– Matthew 3:16-17*

Children occupy a special place in the hearts of their parents.
Watching my three sons grow and mature and have families of
their own has brought me great joy. Countless photo albums and
picture frames document the fun, laughter, and milestones of my
family, which now includes grandchildren and great-grandchildren.

When we receive Christ, we become children of God. At His
baptism, as Jesus identified with our sin and began His ministry
on earth, God the Father's voice is heard expressing His love and
delight in His Son. Because we are His children, God the Father
delights in us, too. That wonderful truth should cause us to
worship and serve God with love and devotion as Jesus did. So
remind yourself often that God delights in you, as you look for
opportunities to serve Him.

Stop Playing God

God's plan for your life is so much better than yours!

The mind of man plans his way,
but the Lord directs his steps.
– Proverbs 16:9

Constant stress is like a stretched-out rubber band. Take a rubber band, stretch it, and leave it stretched for longer and longer periods of time. Eventually it will snap, or it will grow weaker and lose its elasticity. This is what can happen to us if we're not careful.

Stress can be a deadly thing. One of the key anti-stressors I know is for us to stop playing God. Stop trying to run your life independent of God. Listen carefully: If you try to be more than you were intended to be, you will be less than you were intended to be. Just take your hands off your life and place it in God's hands instead. He's got the winning recipe for your life, so turn it over to Him and stop playing God.

A Second Chance

**Through the good news of Jesus,
we can have a second chance in life.**

*But as many as received Him, to them He gave the
right to become children of God, even to those who
believe in His name, who were born, not of blood nor
of the will of the flesh nor the will of man, but of God.*
– John 1:12-13

U.S. Navy Captain Tom Joyce survived the 9/11 terrorist attack on the Pentagon. When he arrived home late that evening, his son said very emotionally, "Dad, I'm so thankful to God that you are alive." After a little while, his son asked, "What are you going to do with the second chance God has given you?" That is a question before all of us. In Christ, God has given us the opportunity of a second chance to live life as He intended.

When we are born again spiritually, we receive a new nature. We become brand new. That's the Good News of the gospel message. Have you received the second chance of the gospel? If so, what are you going to do with it?